MW01168373

Harnessing T

In The Beginning God

By

Marier Farley

Copyright © 2017 All Right Reserved.

Scriptures taken from the Holy Bible, New International Version®. NIV®.
Copyright © 1973, 1978, 1984, 2011 by Biblica, Inc.™ Used by permission of Zondervan.
All rights reserved worldwide www.zondervan.com The "NIV" and "New International
Version" are trademarks registered in the United States Patent and Trademark Office by Biblica,
Inc.™

No part of this publication may be reproduced, distributed, or transmitted in any form or
by any means, including photocopying, recording, or other electronic or mechanical methods, or by
any information storage and retrieval system without the prior written
permission of the publisher, except in the case of very brief quotations embodied in critical reviews
and certain other noncommercial uses permitted by copyright law.

Dedication

This book is dedicated to the ladies in green, Lula B Edwards, a beloved aunt and Brenda Joyce Logan Turner Hughes a beloved sister-in-law. Both of these ladies lost the battle with illness the first to a stroke and the second to bone cancer, but they won the war because they are home with our Lord and Savior Jesus the Christ. I will see you again.

This book was published thanks to free support and training from:

EbookPublishingSchool.com

Find me at www.marierfarley.com

Acknowledgement

I would like to thank F. H. Blocker, S. N. Patterson, D. J. Patterson II, V. Z. H. Hughes, K. J. and N. J. Hughes, V. P. Hughes, Y. R. Hughes, R. E. Hughes, and D. Patterson for helping me get finished with this book. Without your encouragement I would've stopped writing. Thank you. Special thanks go to my special sister who went on my first date with me at the age of 3 as my chaperone, M. M. D. Hughes. She will always hold a special place in my heart. She died at the age of 4.

Table of Contents

Contents

INTRODUCTION

Over my lifetime, I have discovered that many churches and religious leaders make praying difficult for the common man. Observing this again and again was quite troubling to me, as prayer should not be hard work. It should be as natural as talking and listening while cooking dinner, working in the garden or driving along the highway.

My findings led me to write this book, as I felt compelled to reinforce the true reasons for praying. Prayer is an important part of the Christian life; we pray in words and in song. It is also an important part of other religious teachings as well.

Prayer is a shield to the soul, a sacrifice to God and a scourge for Satan.

– John Bunyan

Prayer is often thought to be a lengthy process including everything and everyone, and constructed to be fervent and full of emotion. In reality, a simple "thank you, Lord" is a prayer. When we pray, we acknowledge there is a power higher than us who will not only listen, but will grant us what we pray for as long as it is within the will of God.

My goal is for this book to help Christians remember who they are praying to, why they pray, what hinders prayer, who they should pray for and how they should pray. I also want them to know what a healthy prayer life is like, and understanding there are ways to continually improve it.

Every one of us can pray. We do not have to be fine orators or have all the right words and intonations. God only requires a willing and believing heart. Prayer is important in the lives of everyone, especially to the Christians who know, trust and believe in the true and living God.

Harnessing the power in prayer is a process that should be done constantly. Having an effective prayer life will not only keep you grounded but should keep you aware of the power of God and how praying for others and yourself will help the world be a better place.

6For in Him all things were created, things in heaven and on earth, visible and invisible, whether thrones or dominions or rulers or authorities. All things were created through Him and for Him. 17Heis before all things, and in Him all things hold together. 18And He is the head of the body, the church; He is the beginning and firstborn from among the dead, so that in all things He may have preeminence....Colossians 1:16-17

Remember in the beginning God.

CHAPTER 1: WHAT DOES IT MEAN TO PRAY?

We live in a complex world of vast diversity, brimming with religious organizations, rhetoric, philosophies and theological principles. It is no wonder it is also filled with a multitude of definitions and descriptions when it comes to prayer. If we are to study and fully understand prayer, it is important to gain a firm grasp of its meaning so we can create a strong foundation for it to take flight.

Taking a look at the legal definition of prayer as recorded in merriamwebster.com/dictionary/prayer, we find this:

> Prayer is **a** (1): an address (as a petition) to God or a god in word or thought said a prayer for the success of the voyage (2): a set order of words used in praying **b**: an earnest request or wish 2: the act or practice of praying to God or a god • kneeling in prayer 3: a religious service consisting chiefly of prayers–often used in plural 4: something prayed for 5: a slight chance • haven't got a prayer

In another popular website, http://www.dictionary.com/browse/prayer, the concept of prayer offers a different approach:

Prayer is defined as 1. a devout petition to God or an object of worship. 2. a spiritual communion with God or an object of worship, as in supplication, thanksgiving, adoration, or confession. 3. the act or practice of praying to God or an object of worship. 4. a formula or sequence of words used in or appointed for praying: The Lord's Prayer. 5. prayers, a religious observance, either public or private, consisting wholly or mainly of prayer. 6. that which is prayed for. 7. a petition; entreaty.

Adding depth to its review, biblestudytools.com/encyclopedias/isbe/prayer.ht ml follows a theological view in its definition of prayer:

Prar (deesis, proseuche, (enteuxis; for an excellent discussion of the meaning of these, see Thayer's Lexicon, p. 126, under the word deesis; the chief verbs are euchomai, proseuchomai, and deomai, especially in Luke and Acts; aiteo,"to ask a favor," distinguished from erotao,"to ask a question," is found occasionally):

In the Bible, "prayer" is used in a simpler yet a more complex manner with, a narrower and a wider signification. In the former case, it is supplication for benefits either for one's self (petition) or for others (intercession). In the latter, it is an act of worship which covers all souls in its approach to God. Supplication is at the heart of it, for prayer always springs out of a sense of need and a belief that God is a rewarder of them that diligently seek Him (Hebrews 11:6). But, adoration and confession and thanksgiving also find its place, so that

4

the supplicant becomes a worshipper. It is unnecessary to distinguish all the various terms for prayer that are employed in the Old Testament and the New Testament. But, the fact should be noted that in the Hebrew and Greek alone, there are, on the one hand, words for prayer that denote a direct petition or short, sharp cry of the heart in its distress (Psalms 30:2; 2 Corinthians 12:8), and on the other, "prayers" like that of Hannah (1 Samuel 2:1-10), which is in reality a song of thanksgiving, or that of Paul, the prisoner of Jesus Christ, in which intercession is mingled with doxology (Ephesians 3:14-21).

In my research of the definition of prayer, I found a more simple, direct meaning. That is, prayer is a communication with God. Communication is a conversation involving talking and listening. You pour out your thanksgiving and praise then your requests and then wait and listen for the answer but you listen with an open heart and mind.

There are those who have problems in knowing if God is answering their prayer or if it is just the way of life. The best way to hear God's voice is to study His Word. All of the answers you are looking for can be found there. You will know that He has answered your prayer because you will have discovered that He always answers prayers.

Prayer is a dialogue, not a monologue. It should be meaningful and righteous. God answers us in many ways and if we know Him and His Word, then we are sure to see the answers. Prayer is a perpetual exercise of faith, the most wonderful act in the spiritual realm, as well as the most mysterious affair. It should always be a part of your life.

"Men ought always to pray and not to faint." (Luke 18:1)

Our prayers must be Spirit-taught. It is impossible for us to agonize in prayer, unless we pray in the Spirit (Jude 20). The Lord Jesus said that the Holy Spirit would teach us all things including how to pray.

"Likewise the Spirit also helpeth our infirmities: for we know not what to pray for as we ought: but the Spirit itself maketh intercession for us with groanings which cannot be uttered." Romans 8:28

Yes, the Holy Spirit helps us to pray aright and leads us into deeper levels of communion with our heavenly Father.

Prayer is a privilege and an obligation of the Christian, where we communicate with God. God wants our communication with Him to be unencumbered. To help us achieve this, He set forth simple guidelines that do not involve a list of rules and regulations. But gives us an example of things that we can and should include in our prayers. If we look at the Model Prayer or what some call The Lord's Prayer, we can see what God expects of us in our prayer life. This is just the model and is not expected to be conformed exactly. As with any model, you can tailor it to your understanding, one that comes from God as you dig into His Word.

Our Father, which art in heaven.

This tells us we have a Father in heaven that we are talking to.

Hallowed be thy Name.

"Hallowed" means holy. We show that God and His name are holy and we must understand that He is faultless and pure actuality.

Thy Kingdom come.

God's ways and orders will happen here on earth and be obeyed as they are in heaven.

Thy will be done in earth, God's will occurs.

We align our will with God's will; we are submitting ourselves to Him.

As it is in heaven.

God's will is obeyed in heaven and we will obey on earth just the same.

Give us this day our daily bread.

We must ask daily for God to fulfill our every need. That is why it is so important to have a daily prayer life. This should include many times a day as often as you need or desire.

"Therefore do not worry about tomorrow, for tomorrow will worry about itself. Each day has enough trouble of its own." Mathew 6:34, NIV

And forgive us our trespasses.

We have sinned and ask God to forgive us.

7

As we forgive them that trespass against us.

We must forgive others because God has forgiven us.

And lead us not into temptation,

We ask for help during temptation. We are always tempted, but we have help to deliver us from the temptation.

But, deliver us from evil.

We are to depend on God to help us when evil comes for us. It helps us know that evil will come in spite of who or what we are. We need God to deliver us from it in His way and His time.

For thine is the kingdom, The power and the glory, for ever and ever. Amen.

In this closing, we acknowledge that the kingdom is God's; He has all power and glory. We praise God in this ending and the Amen is telling God that we agree with Him and His word.

This model exhibits several key areas we should include in our prayers.

A. Recognize God as our father.

B. Honor Him and His ways.

C. Ask for forgiveness with the belief and expectation of receiving it.

D. Forgive others.

E. Ask for deliverance.

F. Give Him recognition for his power, glory and kingdom.

Do you realize that even directing a thought toward God qualifies as silent prayer? It is true! Whether you have prayed for years, are just learning to pray, have hit a "slump" in your spiritual life or simply want your prayer life to improve, know this: God wants you to learn to pray more effectively, and He wants your prayer life to become more fulfilling.

DISCUSSION QUESTIONS

1. What is your definition of prayer?
2. Why do you need to search the scriptures to discover effective praying?
3. Is a simple prayer just as effective as a long prayer? Why or why not?
4. Why is prayer a dialogue and not a monologue?
5. Should all prayers follow the model or The Lord's Prayer? Why or why not?
6. Why is daily prayer a must to have a complete prayer life?

CHAPTER 2: WHY SHOULD YOU PRAY?

It is not a hard question. But, it is one that overflows with countless answers. Why should you pray? Is it to get that big promotion? To heal a sick family member? To ask for forgiveness? All of the above are certainly reasons why we pray. Yet, there is only one answer that holds true as to why you should pray.

Prayer is a commandment of God.

God has commanded us to pray to Him and to Him alone. In times of distress, we must turn to God for help. In times of comfort, we must express our gratitude to God. And; and when all goes well with us, we must still pray to God daily that He continues to show us His mercy and grant us our daily needs.

"Watch and pray so that you will not fall into temptation. The spirit is willing, but the flesh is weak." Matthew 26: 41

According to this scripture, you are not only commanded to pray but to watch. When you watch, you first make sure you know the will of God and, second, you watch so that you do not go against the will of God. As referenced in Chapter 1, the Holy Spirit teaches you to pray. So, when you remain in the spirit of God, you pray as you should.

"Only ask, and I will give you the nations as your inheritance, the ends of the earth as your possession." Psalms 2:8, NLT

This scripture seems to clearly state that God is talking to His Son and not to the rest of us. Yet, we are compelled to pray for one another. By reading the whole Bible and applying it to your prayer life, you will realize that according to Romans 8:16-17, any promise God gave to His Son is ours as well. We are co-heirs with Christ of all the Father has given Him.

> *"The Spirit himself testifies with our spirit that we are God's children. Now if we are children, then we are heirs–heirs of God and co-heirs with Christ." Romans. 8:16-17, NIV*

The New Living Translation reads:

> *"Everything God gives to His Son, Christ, is ours, too."*

Keeping these scriptures in your heart helps you understand that you are not only required to pray for yourself, family, friends and church members but for all of the nations of the world. They are your inheritance.

For many people, prayer provides a specialized ministry when other popular callings may seem out of reach. Everyone has their own calling. An effective prayer life may be what God has called you to have. We cannot all be pastors, teachers, missionaries, choir members, deacons or deaconesses, ambassadors, leaders, apostles, prophets, evangelists or elders. Ephesians 4:10-13 He who descended is the very one who ascended higher than all the heavens, in order to fill the whole universe.) 11And it was He who gave some to be apostles, some to be prophets, some to be evangelists, and some to be pastors and teachers, 12to equip the saints for works of ministry, to build up the body of Christ, 13until we all reach unity in the faith and in the knowledge of the Son of God, as we mature to the full measure of the stature of Christ.

But, we can all have an effective prayer life that involves praying for others.

When we embark on an effective prayer life, we can do two things that prayer is designed to fulfill.

1. **We minister to the Lord.** This concerns our personal worship focusing on a passion for the Lord.

2. **We minister to others.** We do this even when we do not have plentiful resources, or are unable to travel and spread the Good News to foreign lands. All we have to do is look at a map and begin praying for a specific region. There is no need to know what is going on in that region–just know that someone there needs you to petition the Father for him or her.

    "Sing a new song to the Lord! Let the whole earth sing to the Lord! Sing to the Lord; bless His name. Each day proclaim the good news that He saves. Publish His glorious deeds among the nations. Tell everyone about the amazing things He does. Tell all the nations that the Lord is king." Psalms 96:1-3; 10, NLT

When Jesus commissioned the 70 to go forth with the gospel, He admonished them:

*"'When you enter a house, first say, 'Peace to this house.'"
Luke 10:5*

Prayer for our neighbors (and nations) is the primary blessing we can give them. Prayer additionally prepares the way for the rest of God's plan to be effective. When we embark on an effective prayer life we know that we must be prepared to pray for others as well as ourselves.

Genuine Preparation

When we intercede in prayer, we plead our case before the eternal judge of the universe. Every case we present to God calls for genuine preparation.

> "Therefore, confess your sins to each other and pray for each other so that you may be healed." James 5:16

The prayer of a righteous person is powerful and effective. For nothing brings man closer to God than prayer, when prayer is truly the outpouring of the soul and, therefore, makes for an "attachment of spirit to spirit." When your spirit aligns with God's spirit, you experience a change in what you are praying for in your own life. Knowing and doing the will of God–which begins with an effective prayer life–is a powerful factor for change.

If we want to effect change in this world, we must first connect with the spirit of God. This connection must be maintained constantly. Sometimes just an acknowledgement that you are lost or confused about something and ask God to help you is an effective prayer. You have acknowledged that God is in control, that you cannot do it and that He is the only one who can help you. This is an extremely effective communication. You have accepted that He will answer in His way and time. That reflects the belief you have in your prayer and in God.

Once you become familiar with God, your prayer life and service becomes even more effective. Prayer is for knowing God and relating to Him in all of life.

DISCUSSION QUESTIONS

1. Why pray at all?
2. What are three reasons why you should pray?
3. What does it mean to have your spirit aligned with God's spirit?
4. What is genuine preparation?
5. What does prayer ministry mean to you?

CHAPTER 3: THE GREAT COMMISSION AND PRAYER

Do you know what the Great Commission is? If you do not know, you may want to find out, as true believers in Jesus are mandated to carry it out. When you begin to carry out this mandate, you see change over the circumstances you are praying for.

A mandate is defined as "a resounding directive" or "a clear and focused objective given by a person or persons in authority." Another definition reads, "To put into one's hands; to command or entrust." We discover our mandate from Christ in such commands.

> "Therefore go and make disciples of all nations...teaching them to obey everything I have commanded you." Matthew 28:19-20, NIV

Luke provides a description of the biblical pattern for fulfilling this mandate when he tells in his gospel how the early church responded to Christ's command.

> "Day after day, in the temple courts and from house to house, they never stopped teaching and proclaiming the good news that Jesus is the Christ." Acts 5:42

Following the Great Commission is a Christion's only true occupation. Everything else is what helps you do this. You are here to spread the Good News of Jesus. Beginning with Genesis 3:15 and the Fall through Adam, we know that all things lead to Christ, the only one who can save us. As joint heirs with Him, we are always compelled to be about our Father's business. We cannot save anyone, but we can point them toward salvation.

The effective prayer of a righteous man can accomplish much. The prayers of the righteous avails much is part of God's Word.

> *James 5:16 Confess your faults one to another, and pray one for another, that ye may be healed. The effectual fervent prayer of a righteous man availeth much.*

Understanding this, we know that we can petition God for what we need and want. He will always answer. It may not be what you want, but it is always the right thing. And remember, human responsibility is included. For your prayers to be effective, you must be righteous.

You are also told to confess your sins. Does this mean you should just start telling everyone your sins? No, you must use discretion and the Word in all that you do. "A righteous man's prayer is so powerful that it moves the hand of Him who moves the world." (http://www.worldinvisible.com/library/bounds/5b b.10597-possibilities/5bb.10597.04.htm)

Confess to your spiritual leader who is obligated to keep your confession secret if you ask. When you confess publicly you may expect some to not understand or ridicule you but remember they are not the ones who will be your final judge. Therefore, do as God says. All have sinned and fallen short of the glory of God. All humans are imperfect beings and if some of them turn away from you they were never meant to be a part of your life anyway. Never allow someone else's reality to define your own, especially if their reality does not line up with God's Word.

Praying for one another is a part of the Great Commission. You cannot spread the Good News effectively if your prayer life is not correct.

Prayer is the belief that God can be asked to change or intervene and that He will. This does not take away from anything that He is. It just allows us, His creatures, to have input in what is going on in our lives. We cannot make God do anything. He already knows what you are going to ask for before you ask. The key here is that you believe in Him enough to ask in the first place.

There are many instances when prayers are answered in ways we do not expect. Perhaps you are praying for healing of a loved one and he or she dies. Does this mean God did not answer your prayer? No, because we humans must die. So, praying for the healing that resulted in a human death, but caused a spiritual healing, for the people who are surrounding the one whose death occurred. The death may have helped open someone's eyes to the fact that God is real and this leads them to Christ.

7"For we walk by faith, not by sight. 8 We are confident, then, and would prefer to be away from the body and at home with the Lord. 9 So, we aspire to please Him, whether we are here in this body or away from it." 2 Corinthians 5:7-8 7

Your confidence must be in God. He gives us example after example in His Word. (Matt 6:913 ;Luke 11:2-4) and in His assurance that one only has to ask the Father to receive what was needed (Matt 7:7 ; Luke 11:9). We can readily document that Jesus' instructions were taken to heart by his early followers: there were prayers for the selection of leaders, for deliverances from prisons, for the spread of the gospel, for healings, and so on (e.g., see Acts 1:24; 12:5 ; 13:3). Indeed, Paul's teaching in Philippians 4:6 echoes Jesus' own. Thus, prayer was unquestioningly believed to be an effective cause of God's actions such that a difference resulted in human events.

In none of these examples do feelings come into play. Feelings can be deceptive and sometimes we must move beyond our feelings to the facts at hand. This is why the Bible is so important–it tells you what God has done and the implications of his actions. Most importantly, it shares His promises and His faithfulness in keeping those promises. While the immanence (God is always present within the universe, though distinct from it. God is 'within' the universe in that God is its sustaining cause. (Geisler) of God formed much of the basis for prayer in the Judeo-Christian tradition, God's transcendence (The transcendence of God is closely related to his sovereignty. It means that God is above, other than, and distinct from all he has made - he transcends it all. Paul says that there is "one God and

18

Father of all, who is over all and through all and in all (Ephesians 4:6).

Scripture says elsewhere, "For you, O LORD, are the Most High over all the earth; you are exalted far above all gods (Psalms 97:9; cf. 108:5). is important as well. God maintains the prerogative of denying the prayer's request. God's hand cannot be forced. In fact, even the intimacy of the "abba" in the Lord's Prayer is mitigated by the following phrase, "who are in heaven," to ensure that petitioners remember they and the addressee are not on a par with each other. God is the Supreme Being or reality, both omnipresent ("This is not to say that God's form is spread out so that parts of Him exist in every location. God is spirit; He has no physical form. He is present everywhere in that everything is immediately in His presence. At the same time He is present everywhere in the universe. No one can hide from Him and nothing escapes His notice.") and omnipotent (All-ruling, "Alleluia! For the Lord God Omnipotent reigns!" (Revelation 19:6). He can perform what is asked, but he stands over against the prayer and, as such, he is sovereign over the petitioner, in providential control of the universe, and the source and bestower of all that we receive.

In all this we the creatures must understand that God the Creator is always in charge and will only what His will says do. This behooves us to learn His will and have our prayers surrounded by this knowledge so being genuine wine in your study of God's Word to make your prayer effective is imperative.

Service is part of the Great Commission in that you have to <u>willingly go and do</u> for others to spread the Good News. Prayer goes hand in hand with service. To fulfill the mandate, we must shoulder the responsibility of going out into unknown territory and tell people about Christ. When you go out into the world, you should be fully equipped. When you put on the full armor of God, The Helmet of Salvation, The Shield of Faith, The Breastplate of Righteousness, The Belt of Truth, The Sword of the Spirit, and include continual and persistent prayer, you go out protected from the evil of the world.

Your service may be that you spend time praying for those who go out to spread the Good News. Perhaps your service is just allowing God to speak through you so that your words will lead people to Christ. Service comes in many forms and just because you can't be on the mission field does not mean you can't serve. Ask God what you can do to serve him he will let you know. Open your heart and mind to actually hear the Word of God.

"The Lord is far from the wicked, but He hears the prayer of the righteous. That means that we must be righteous when we pray." Proverbs 15:29

DISCUSSION QUESTIONS

1. Does praying take anything away from God and who and what He is?
2. Name three ways that you can know your prayers are answered.
3. What does repenting and relenting mean in relation to how God answers prayers?
4. Why do feelings have nothing to do with how God answers our prayers?
5. Why does fulfilling the mandate of the Great Commission always involve a prayer life?

CHAPTER 4: WHAT IS VAIN REPETITION?

Matthew 6:7

In praying, do not babble like the pagans, who think that they will be heard because of their many words. (NABRE)

But when ye pray, use not vain repetitions, as the heathen do: for they think that they shall be heard for their much speaking. (KJV)

And when you pray, do not keep on babbling like pagans, for they think they will be heard because of their many words. (NIV)

And in praying do not heap up empty phrases as the Gentiles do; for they think that they will be heard for their many words. (RSV)

And when you are praying, speak not much, as the heathens. For they think that in their much speaking they may be heard. (DRA)

Matthew 6:7-8

But thou, when thou prayest, enter into thy closet, and when thou hast shut thy door, pray to thy Father which is in secret; and thy Father which seeth in secret shall reward thee openly. 7But when ye pray, use not vain repetitions, as the heathen do: for they think that they shall be heard for their much speaking. 8 Be not ye therefore like unto them: for your Father knoweth what things ye have need of, before ye ask him.

I Kings 18 is an example of "vain repetitions." The prophets of Baal tried to make their altar ignite by dancing around it, chanting, screaming to their gods and injuring themselves. This went on for several hours before Elijah calmly and publicly asked God to show Himself and burn up His sacrifice–which He did. Baal's prophets kept repeating the same thing only louder, but they were believing in their prayer rather than who they were praying to. Baal was also a statue and could not hear them. But, Elijah was praying to the true and most important living God who heard his prayer and answered it. Such a difference between vain repetition and prayer must be noted.

Take a look at what John says in chapter 14, telling us what Jesus said.

> And whatever you ask in My name, that I will do, that the Father may be glorified in the Son. 14 If you ask anything in My name, I will do it. 15 "If you love Me, keep My commandments. 16 And I will pray the Father, and He will give you another Helper, that He may abide with you forever. John 14:13-16:

Prayer without faith is in vain. When you pray, you must pray with the expectation that God will answer your prayer according to His will and timing. You must have faith in God and in knowing your prayer will be heard and answered. God delights in our prayer, even though He knows what you need before you ask. He delights in knowing that you love, respect and have enough faith in Him to come to His throne of grace and make a petition to Him. Jesus did not ask us to pray for the sake of praying as a Christian routine, but He asks us to pray so that we can receive. You will not pray vain repetition even when you repeat yourself. Your prayer will be embedded with faith in Jesus that He hears and answers prayer.

> Until now you have asked nothing in My name. Ask, and you will receive, that your joy may be full." John 16:24

This is another promise that you must not pray vain prayers nor prayers that go against the will of God. When you ask in faith, you will know that God is going to answer your prayers. You will know that His answer is the correct one and that nothing can change how He feels about you. When your prayers are in the will of God, even though they may seem to be selfish prayers to you, God hears and answers them.

In Christianity, our faith does not depend on our prayer but on the God who answers the prayer. Christ did not teach us to put our faith in our prayer, but in God that answers prayer; He said we should even believe God's answers before praying. So, "It is not by power, neither by might, but by My Spirit" says the Lord.

> Then he answered and spoke unto me, saying, "This is the word of the Lord unto Zerubbabel, saying, 'Not by might nor by power, but by My Spirit,' saith the Lord of hosts. Zechariah 4:6

The heathens' faith is hinged on their prayer, believing the answers to their prayers are determined by their prayer, "For they think that they will be heard for their many words."

> And when you pray, do not keep on babbling like pagans, for they think they will be heard because of their many words. Matthew 6:7

Vain repetition is more serious, subtle and deceptive. There is a difference between "vain repetition" and "repetition" Jesus prayed three times at Gethsemane and repeated the same prayer points. Jesus did not say we should not repeat or re-emphasize in our prayers. He did not oppose repetition, but only "vain" repetition. When you send a bold, but humble prayer in faith heavenward, you can repeat it as often as you must until you get the answer. It does not mean you cannot pray more than once for the same thing. Jesus says "knock"–and keep knocking. Prayer should be made continuously without ceasing. In any particular request, we should keep asking until our joy is full–that is faith repetition, not vain repetition. Keep the Word of God in total obedience, keep the faith and keep praying until your joy is full.

http://www.gospelchapel.com/Devotions/11_98/devotion_11-04-98.html

When considering vain repetition, think praying just to impress the audience are praying so that people will say that you pray quick prayers. The whole goal of vain repetition is not for the content of the prayer book words that make the person talking sound good.

DISCUSSION QUESTIONS

1. What does vain repetition mean to you? Give an example.
2. Why did Jesus warn against vain repetition?
3. Do you think asking God over and over for the same thing is vain repetition? Why or why not?
4. What does John 14:13-16 mean to you?
5. Why is it important to have faith when praying?

CHAPTER 5: WHAT HINDERS PRAYER?

"O God, hear my prayer; give ear to the words of my mouth." Psalm 54:2

Hinder means to delay, deter, hamper, encumber, obstruct, thwart, impede, hold back or get in the way. All of these demonstrate the negative in this world. You are the only one who can hinder your prayers. When we allow something to hinder our prayer life, we allow the enemy to come in and steal our joy.

In truth, our prayers are often hindered. While we can be sure that God does hear our prayers, there are times when He chooses not to heed or answer them. God sometimes delays His answers so that we will diligently seek Him and learn how to be patient.

With that said, would you purposely hinder your prayer life? Probably not. However, you may be doing just that if you think your prayers are not getting through or you have other negative thoughts about your prayer life. You may hinder your prayers even when you think you are doing everything right.

As you journey through this chapter, think about each individual hindrance to your prayer life. Then find a way to expel them so you can be an effective person of prayer.

What hinders prayer? When you think about prayers and what can stop them, do you think about God not listening or, perhaps, you not correctly communicating? Is your lack of faith hindering your prayers? Are you so busy that you do not have time to stop and listen? Do you allow life to get in the way of your prayers? These are just a few ways that hinder prayer. Maybe you are asking outside of God's will, or you are asking for something you do not need or can't handle right now. In your dialogue with God, think about what could be hindering your prayer and write your prayers down, asking God for understanding.

Remember, this is a conversation between you and God, and you must wait and listen. Sometimes He answers "yes," Other times, "no." And, of course, He also can answer "wait." Do not let this get in the way of your own prayers. God will answer the prayer; it just may not be the reply you are hoping for. But, He answers.

Let's take a look at a few ways we hinder prayer and why they get in the way of your dialogue with God. Then we will look at how you can change, correct or remove these for a more fervent and effective prayer life.

DISOBEDIENCE

Chances are you learned first-hand about disobedience in your childhood, perhaps being reprimanded by your parents for not doing as you were told. Disobedience also means defiance, noncompliance, insubordination, naughtiness, waywardness, rebellion and breaking the rules. Clearly, these are all negative actions – prime tools for Satan. To be righteous in prayer, you must be obedient. And the only way to be obedient to God is to study His Word.

> *"And whatever we ask we receive from Him, because we keep His commandments and do those things which are pleasing in His sight." 1John 3:22*

SELFISH MOTIVES

All humans are selfish. It is part of our human nature to naturally regard our own interests ahead of the interests of others. Sadly, we often regard our own interests ahead of God's.

We must ask in accordance with God's will as revealed in the Bible. We must ask only for things that are consistent with the character and nature of God. We must ask for things that are for the spiritual benefit of ourselves or for the ones we pray for. God does not answer self-centered, self-serving prayers.

Ask for the things in God's will, where the outcome of which is to honor and glorify Him. "You ask and do not receive because you ask amiss, that you may spend it on your pleasures." James 4:3

Are your prayers selfish? Not to say you should never pray for yourself, but your prayers for yourself should be carried out in God's will, bringing Him glory. Any blessing that is bestowed upon you must be so you can bless others. You do not have to give it all away. Only, share your blessing.

UNCONFESSED SIN

There is no doubt that sin—what we have refused to confess before God—hinders our prayers.

> 8"If I had cherished iniquity in my heart, the Lord would not have listened" (Psalm 66:18), says the Psalmist. Romans 5:8-10. 8But God proves His love for us in this: While we were still sinners, Christ died for us. 9Therefore, since we have now been justified by His blood, how much more shall we be saved from wrath through Him 10For if, when we were enemies of God, we were reconciled to Him through the death of His Son, how much more, having been reconciled, shall we be saved through His life!

You must examine your heart closely to determine if there is unconfessed sin in your life. Sometimes that sin can even be self-directed. If you sinned in the past and confessed it, asking for forgiveness, and yet you still beat yourself up over it, then that is still sin. You have not accepted God's will over that sin. He said He is faithful and just to forgive.

> "If we confess our sins, he is faithful and just and will forgive us our sins and purify us from all unrighteousness. He will cast that sin into the sea." 1 John 1:9

> "You will again have compassion on us; you will tread our sins underfoot and hurl all our iniquities into the depths of the sea." Micah 7:19

But you swim out there and go pick it back up again. Either you trust God to do as He said He would do, or you don't. The latter of the two behaviors can hinder your prayer life.

While we should continually examine our hearts, we also need to ask God to reveal our sin to us. We should ask those closest to us what they have observed in our lives. While God most often reveals sin through the reading of and meditating upon His Word, we should realize that if we do not learn our lesson from Scripture, He may have to resort to harsher tactics where our sin is revealed before others, even publicly. While this may be difficult and humiliating, He does so because He loves us and does not wish for this sin to continue to corrupt us and to stand as a barrier between Himself and us.

FAILURE TO ASK GOD TO SUPPLY OUR NEEDS

"You lust and do not have. You murder and covet and cannot obtain. You fight and war. Yet you do not have because you do not ask." James 4:2 says

God will supply all of our needs according to His riches... And my God will meet all your needs according to the riches of his glory in Christ Jesus." Philippians 4:19

These two scriptures help us know our needs will be met and that we must ask God to meet them. We are unable to do it alone. The job opportunity is provided by God. We are steered in the direction He wants us to go if we put our faith in Him. Have you asked God to supply your needs? Notice that it says needs–not wants. God is so good that He always supplies our needs. But, He also gives us some of our wants as well. He understands us so well that He knows we have needs and wants. He provides them according to His will.

Don't let lusts for things that other people have cause your prayer life to suffer. Trust God to supply your every need. Being poor does not mean you do not have God's favor, nor does being rich mean you do have His favor. God knows you and what you can handle. He promised to always be with you.

FORGETTING THE POOR

Ignoring and not having compassion

"Whoever shuts his ears to the cry of the poor will also cry himself and not be heard." Proverbs 21:13

What a powerful verse! Have you ever seen someone in need and you did nothing to help him, even though you had the power? Do you give to your church according to how God has blessed you, or is the church the last bill you pay when all else has been covered? Those of us who are blessed with wealth beyond our need have a responsibility to share generously with the less fortunate. We should view our wealth as a gift from God, entrusted to us, to carry out His work on earth.

"If anyone has material possessions and sees his brother in need but has no pity on him, how can the love of God be in him?" NIV, 1 John 3:17

"Command those who are rich in this present world not to be arrogant nor to put their hope in wealth, which is so uncertain, but to put their hope in God, who richly provides us with everything for our enjoyment. Command them to do good, to be rich in good deeds, and to be generous and willing to share. In this way they will lay up treasure for themselves as a firm

31

foundation for the coming age, so that they may take hold of the life that is truly life." (NIV, 1 Timothy 6:17-19)

Any blessing that you have must be shared. It is not to be stored away, especially when you can help others. You are also to be wise in how you deal with your sharing. Do not get so caught up in helping others that you neglect your family or yourself. You are commanded to do good, not to make a complete sacrifice that you are left suffering and your bills are not paid. If you give to God according to how you have been blessed, then He will bless what is left to supply your needs. Remember the poor, and it will not be a hindrance to your prayer life.

DOUBT OR UNBELIEF

Pray with confidence, believing God to do what He said He will do.

> *"But let him ask in faith, with no doubting, for he who doubts is like a wave of the sea driven and tossed by the wind. For let not that man suppose that he will receive anything from the Lord." James 1:6-7*

Doubt is a major hindrance to your prayer life. When you consider that doubt means uncertainty, misgiving, distrust, disbelief, suspicion and skepticism, you will see why your prayer life is hindered. God wants us to have confidence in His ability and willingness to provide what is necessary for us to attain godliness. He wants us to believe He can and will do what He says. Thus, when we doubt– when we ask expecting rejection and when we ask almost hoping for rejection–we hinder our prayers.

> "If any of you lacks wisdom, let him ask God, who gives generously to all without reproach, and it will be given him. But let him ask in faith, with no doubting, for the one who doubts is like a wave of the sea that is driven and tossed by the wind. For that person must not suppose that he will receive anything from the Lord." James 1:5-7

Our prayers cannot be separated from our faith. If we are to ask God, we must ask with expectancy, believing in our heart of hearts that God can and will give what we desire, provided that what we desire is really what we need and what will bring glory to Him! We are to ask with confidence and expectancy, praying out of the faith He has given us. Never let doubt or unbelief get in the way of your relationship with God and your dialogue with Him.

DISHARMONY IN FAMILY OR WIH OTHERS

Consider the word disharmony and what it can do to your family, friends and associates. In a word, it means conflict, disagreement, tension, unrest, bitterness, resentment, discord and even cacophony–a loud noise that is off key and causes the ear to hurt. Now imagine how your prayer life suffers when you begin to pray and the family squabble enters your mind, removing whatever you were going to pray from the forefront of your mind. All of a sudden you are not praying. Instead, you are either angry about the situation or wondering what you can do to fix it. Your prayers are now hindered. You must be at peace with one another.

"Husbands, likewise, dwell with them with understanding, giving honour to the wife, as to the weaker vessel, and as being heirs together of the grace of life, that your prayers may not be hindered." 1 Peter 3:7

It is God's will that families live together in peace and harmony. It is, of course, impossible for us to live in perfect peace, but God demands that we maintain close relationships and that we seek harmony in our family relationships. It is foremost the responsibility of the father, as the head of the household, to ensure that there is not discord within the family. When this discord exists, especially in the relationship of a husband to his wife, his prayers may well be hindered. The apostle Peter, a married man himself, exhorted husbands to live with their wives in an understanding way, being sensitive to their needs,

The relationship between husband and wife is to reflect that of Christ to His church. It is to be a relationship of absolute love, adoration and sacrifice. If Christ gave His life for the church, how can a husband do any less for his wife? This is, of course, impossible when the relationship is strained or broken. Thus, a man should examine his relationship with his wife to ensure this is not a hindrance to his prayers (and to hers).

Likewise the relationship with children, neighbors and the rest of the world must be considered and reconciled.

1Children, obey your parents in the Lord, for this is right. 2 "Honor your father and mother"—which is the first commandment with a promise— 3 "so that it may go well with you and that you may enjoy long life on the earth."

Fathers,[b] do not exasperate your children; instead, bring them up in the training and instruction of the Lord.

Slaves, obey your earthly masters with respect and fear, and with sincerity of heart, just as you would obey Christ. 6 Obey them not only to win their favor when their eye is on you, but as slaves of Christ, doing the will of God from your heart. 7 Serve wholeheartedly, as if you were serving the Lord, not people, 8 because you know that the Lord will reward each one for whatever good they do, whether they are slave or free.

9 And masters, treat your slaves in the same way. Do not threaten them, since you know that he who is both their Master and yours is in heaven, and there is no favoritism with him. Ephesians 6:1-9

UNFORGIVING HEARTS

If we do not forgive others, our Heavenly Father will not forgive us. Matthew 6:15

The Christian has been forgiven for the greatest of offenses. He has been forgiven for knowingly, purposely and unrepentantly transgressing the Law of God. And, yet, we are often slow to forgive our fellow man for the smallest of transgressions. Even the biggest of the sins committed against us are nothing compared to how we sinned against God. God does not honor this attitude. Jesus said,

"And whenever you stand praying, forgive, if you have anything against anyone, so that your Father also who is in heaven may forgive you your trespasses." Mark 11:25

When our hearts are hardened toward others, we are saying to God that we dislike His creation. A hard heart does not allow God to work in it. Think about a hard brick. It takes a lot of effort to break it. When you harden your heart, it takes a lot of effort to break through the resentment, anger, hatred and dislike. God has to work through the hardened heart to get to the prayers you are sending His way. This is not an impossibility. It will just cause Him to work on you before He can work through you. If you want your prayers to get through your heart must be open to others as well as to God. A closed hand does not provide room for anything to get in. The same is true of a hardened heart. If it is closed off to others, then you don't have time for God because you are so busy being angry with others. Practice forgiveness daily. Always try to live peacefully with everyone you encounter.

IDOLS

Not putting God first in our lives.

"And the word of the Lord came to me, saying, 'Son of man, these men have set up their idols in their hearts, and put before them that which causes them to stumble into iniquity. Should I let Myself be inquired of by them? Therefore speak to them, 'Thus says the Lord God: 'Everyone of the house of Israel who sets up his idols in his heart, and puts before him what causes him to stumble into iniquity, and then comes to the prophet, I the Lord will answer him who comes, according to the multitude of his idols, that I may seize the house of Israel by their heart, because they are all estranged from Me by their idols.'" Ezekiel 14:2-5 says

You may think this is an easy one to avoid and overcome. Perhaps you do not worship idols such as statues, but you do you make an idol of your car, your home or your children? This happens when you put them all in front of God. Think on the story of Martha and Mary, Lazarus' sisters.

> "She [Martha] had a sister called Mary, who also sat at Jesus' feet and heard His word. But Martha was distracted with much serving, and she approached Him and said, 'Lord, do You not care that my sister has left me to serve alone? Therefore tell her to help me.' And Jesus answered and said to her, 'Martha, Martha, you are worried and troubled about many things. But one thing is needed, and Mary has chosen that good part, which will not be taken from her'." Luke 10:39-42

Martha was doing good, but she put feeding, cooking and cleaning before Jesus. This is not to say to neglect any of these things, but if you miss church or are late for church because you were so busy cooking, cleaning, and washing your car or any other domestic chore, then you have made it an idol. Also, if you don't do what is required of you in raising your children because they did not want to go or do something, you have made idols of them. This will hinder your prayer life. Whatever you put ahead of God becomes an idol. Carefully examine your life to ensure that God is first and everything elses comes behind Him.

LACK OF RECONCILIATION

Bearing malice, hate or grudge

> "Therefore, if you bring your gift to the altar, and there remember that your brother has something against you, leave your gift there before the altar, and go your way. First be

reconciled to your brother, and then come and offer your gift."
Matthew 5:23,24

According to the Bible, reconciliation is a ministry where every believer in the Lord Jesus Christ should engage with the Holy Spirit as the chief guide in this aspect of ministry.

Reconciliation has to do with bringing back together a relationship or mending a broken relationship.

God has gifted us with the ability to mend our broken relationship with him and with others through his Son, Jesus Christ. What many of us do not recognize is the need for mending or that it is possible. After you have accepted Christ as Savior, you may still do something that is against the will of God and conclude it is unforgiveable. Do not let the lack of reconciliation hinder your prayer life. You alone are in control of your ability to reconcile. All you can control is your actions. Ensure that you have sought reconciliation.

PRAYING ALONE

Pray with others and agree in faith.

"Again I say to you that if two of you agree on earth concerning anything that they ask, it will be done for them by My Father in heaven." Matthew 18:19

Public and private prayer are both important. Praying with someone does not have to mean you and that person are in the same place or in direct communication with each other. You can be a volunteer prayer warrior for your church and pray with another group throughout the week for those who request prayer. This group prays at their own time yet they are praying for the request submitted to the group. You can also work with another person and ask him or her to pray with you for a situation. I encourage you to pray with and for others daily. As the scripture indicates, when two agree on earth, God grants it in heaven. We must always remember that what he grants is always in His will.

> *"Again, truly I tell you that if two of you on earth agree about anything they ask for, it will be done for them by my Father in heaven." Matthew 18:19*

AN UNTHANKFUL HEART

Give God thanks in all things, because in all trials, painful situations, He is always with us.

> *"...in everything give thanks; for this is the will of God in Christ Jesus for you." 1 Thessalonians 5:18*

Getting so busy asking God for things, healing, relief from trials and whatever else we ask in our prayer life is a hindrance. We must not just think of God as a Father with deep pockets. We must come to Him in faith and with a thankful heart. We must know that even if He does not answer our prayers like we expect Him to, we must have a thankful heart knowing that He is doing what is best for us. Also, being secure in the knowledge that He can do anything and that failure is never an option for God.

If we do not spend time immersing ourselves in Scripture and are not obeying what we have learned, we should not expect God to answer our prayers. Our defiance in ignoring the life-giving Words of the Bible may hinder us from having our prayers answered. Solomon goes so far as to suggest that prayers made from such a hardened heart are an abomination to God.

> *"If one turns away his ear from hearing the law, even his prayer is an abomination." Proverbs 28:9*

We pray best and most effectively when we are saturated in the Word of God.

When we read the Words of Scripture, we ask and encourage God to speak to us. He provides the understanding we need to live lives that bring glory to Him—lives that are increasingly consistent with His standards of grace and holiness. If we thumb our nose at the importance of this discipline and if we disobey what He teaches, He will not answer our prayers. Without submitting ourselves to Scripture, we may not even know what and how to pray. We pray best and most effectively when we are saturated in the Word of God.

NOT WANTING TO WAIT ON GOD

> *"Ask, and it will be given to you; seek and you will find; knock and it will be opened to you. For everyone who asks receives, and he who seeks finds, and to him who knocks it will be opened." Matthew 7:7,8*

The Holy Spirit can lead us, teach us and guide us to overcome these hindrances, if we ask Him to help us in our daily Christian walk with Jesus Christ. But we must ensure that the voice answering is God's and not our own or Satan's. To do this you must immerse yourself into the scriptures so that when you are presented with half-truths or falsehoods proclaiming to be the scripture you will know the difference.

DISCUSSION QUESTIONS

1. What are three things that hinder prayer? Explain how they hinder prayer.
2. Why does an unforgiving heart hinder prayer?
3. What can you do to ensure that you are not praying alone?
4. How does forgetting the poor create a disconnect between you and God?
5. Why should you wait on the answers from God?
6. Can you think of other ways that prayers can be hindered? If so, what are they?
7. How does an unthankful heart hinder prayer? Explain your answer thoroughly.

CHAPTER 6: REASONS FOR PRAYING

Now that you know how to avoid hindrance of prayer, you can dig further to find the reason for prayer. While there are many reasons to explore, we uncover a few of them here–and you may even add some of your own.

Intercessory Prayer

Intercessory prayer is prayer for others. An intercessor is someone who takes the place of another or pleads another's case. This type of prayer is persevering prayer when someone pleads with God on behalf of another or others who desperately need God's intervention. Intercessory prayer is Biblically based in the Old and New Testaments.

In the Old Testament, the Levites were the priests for the Israelites. The priest's responsibility was to stand before and between. He stood before God to minister to Him with sacrifices and offerings. The priests also stood between a righteous God and sinful man, bringing them together at the place of the blood sacrifice. The Word of God declares that we are a holy priesthood (1 Peter 2:4), a royal priesthood (1 Peter 2:9), and a kingdom of priests (Revelation 1:5). Therefore, we are called to intercede on others' behalf.

Hebrews 7:11-19 explains the difference between the Old and New Testament ministries of the priest. The Old Testament Levitical priesthood was passed on from generation to generation through the descendants of the tribe of Levi. "The Melchizedek priesthood" spoken of in this passage, is the "new order" of spiritual priests of whom the Lord Jesus is the High Priest. It is passed on to us through His blood and our spiritual birth as new creatures in Christ.

Peter uses two words to describe this priestly ministry: "Holy" and "royal." Holiness is required to stand before the Lord (Hebrews 12:14). We are able to do this only on the basis of the righteousness of Christ, not our own righteousness. Royalty is descriptive of the kingly authority that is delegated to us as members of the "royal family," so to speak, with legitimate access to the throne room of God.

Many times, our prayers include requests for others as we intercede for them. We are told to make intercession "for everyone" in 1 Timothy 2:1. Jesus serves as our example in this area. The whole of John 17 is a prayer of Jesus on behalf of His disciples and all believers.

The Bible also speaks of praying in the Spirit (1 Corinthians 14:14-15) and prayers when we are unable to think of adequate words (Romans 8:26-27). In those times, the Spirit Himself makes intercession for us. Prayer is a conversation with God and should be made without ceasing (1 Thessalonians 5:16-18). As we grow in our love for Jesus Christ, we will naturally desire to talk to Him.

Prayer of Salvation

It is important to remember that salvation is not received by reciting a prayer. Salvation is only through faith in Jesus Christ.

> *"For God so loved the world that he gave his one and only Son, that whoever believes in him shall not perish but have eternal life." John 3:16*

Salvation is gained by faith (Ephesians 2:8), by receiving Jesus as Savior (John 1:12), and by fully trusting Jesus alone (John 14:6; Acts 4:12). Once you have gained knowledge about Jesus, you may start a dialogue with God concerning this knowledge, possibly leading to your salvation. But, God put only one stipulation on all humans who wants salvation and that is to receive Jesus as their savior and place their faith in Him.

Sinner's Prayer

The sinner's prayer is when a person prays to God when they understand they are a sinner and in need of a Savior. Saying a sinner's prayer will not accomplish anything on its own. A true sinner's prayer only represents what a person knows, understands and believes about their sinfulness and the need for salvation. To pray this type of prayer, the person must first understand he or she is a sinner.

> *"As it is written, there is none righteous, no, not one." Romans 3:10*

44

We are all sinners in need of mercy and forgiveness from God (Titus 3:5-7). Because of our sin, we deserve eternal punishment (Matthew 25:46). They must then understand what God has put in place to save us from our sins. God took on flesh and became a human being in the Person of Jesus Christ (John 1:1,14). Jesus taught us the truth about God and lived a perfectly righteous and sinless life (John 8:46; 2 Corinthians 5:21). Jesus then died on the cross in our place, taking the punishment that we deserve (Romans 5:8). Jesus rose from the dead to prove His victory over sin, death, and hell (Colossians 2:15; 1 Corinthians chapter 15). All we have to do is believe that He died in our place and rose from the dead (Romans 10:9-10). We can be saved by grace alone, through faith alone, in Jesus Christ alone.

"For it is by grace you have been saved, through faith–and this not from yourselves, it is the gift of God." Ephesians 2:8

Corporate Prayer

Corporate prayer is a vital part of worship. When a group of Christians engages in corporate prayer, they are engaging in an activity that will help those praying, while also helping those who struggle with problems they do not know how to voice. When we pray for all those present, we provide encouragement and the knowledge that someone else is interceding on their behalf.

An important part of the life of the church, along with worship, sound doctrine, communion and fellowship, is corporate prayer. This follows what (Acts

2:42) says. By praying together with other believers, we help lift the most powerful weapon in the universe up to the God of the universe. We glorify God and help edify the church. Prayer, then, is cooperating with God to bring about His plan, not trying to bend Him to our will. As we abandon our own desires in submission to the One who knows our circumstances far better than we ever could and who "knows what you need before you ask" (Matthew 6:8), our prayers reach their highest level. Prayers offered in submission to the Divine will, therefore, are always answered positively, whether offered by one person or a thousand.

Corporate prayer is important because it creates unity.

> 22"I have given them the glory that you gave me, that they may be one as we are one— 23 I in them and you in me–so that they may be brought to complete unity. Then the world will know that you sent me and have loved them even as you have loved me and is a key aspect of believers' encouraging one another." John 17:22-23

> "Therefore encourage one another and build each other up, just as in fact you are doing, and spurring one another on to love and good deeds." 1 Thessalonians 5:11

> "And let us consider how we may spur one another on toward love and good deeds." Hebrews 10:24

After Jesus' ascension, the disciples "all joined together constantly in prayer" (Acts 1:14). Later, after Pentecost, the early church "devoted themselves" to prayer (Acts 2:42). Their example encourages us to pray with others.

We are to come to God in humility (James 4:10), truth (Psalm 145:18), obedience (1 John 3:2122), with thanksgiving (Philippians 4:6) and confidence (Hebrews 4:16).

Imprecatory Prayer

To imprecate means "to invoke evil upon or curse" one's enemies. King David, the psalmist most associated with imprecatory verses such as Psalm 55:15, 69:28, and 109:8, often used phrases like:

"May their path be dark and slippery, with the angel of the LORD pursuing them." Psalm 35:6

"O God, break the teeth in their mouths; tear out the fangs of the young lions, O LORD!" Psalm 58:6.

Psalms 7, 35, 55, 58, 59, 69, 109, and 139 were written by David to ask God to bring judgment upon his enemies. (The other two imprecatory psalms, 79 and 137, were written by Asaph and an unknown psalmist.) These prayers were written not so much to exact revenge upon one's enemies, but rather to emphasize God's abhorrence of evil, His sovereignty over all mankind and His divine protection of His chosen people. Many of these prayers were prophetic and could be seen taking place later in the New Testament in actual historical events.

When David prayed for God to shatter the teeth of his enemies, likening them to young lions pursuing him to his death, he was making the point that God is holy, righteous and just, and He will ultimately judge the wicked for the evil they do. Jesus quoted some of the imprecatory psalms during His earthly ministry. In John 15:25, Jesus quotes Psalm 35:19 and 69:4. Paul also quoted an imprecatory prayer in Romans 11:9–10, which is a quote of Psalm 69:22–23. Since Jesus and Paul quoted verses from these imprecatory psalms, it proves those psalms were inspired by God and counters any allegation that they were sinful or selfish prayers of revenge.

Using imprecatory prayers from Psalms today should only be done against our spiritual enemies (Ephesians 6:12). Praying imprecations on human foes is unjustifiable, as it would require taking these prayers out of context. In the New Testament, Jesus exhorts us to pray for our enemies (Matthew 5:44–48; Luke 6:27–38), but praying for their death or for bad things to happen to them is not what He meant. Instead, we are to pray for their salvation first and foremost, and then for God's will to be done. There's no greater blessing than a personal relationship with Jesus Christ, and that is what Jesus means by praying for and blessing those who curse us.

Praying in that manner allows God to work in our own lives to soften our hearts toward our enemies so that we have compassion on them for their eternal destiny, and to remove bitterness and anger from our hearts. Praying for God's will to be done means we agree with God and are submitting ourselves to His divine sovereignty, despite not always understanding perfectly what He is doing in a particular situation. It also means we have given up the idea that we know best and now rely on and trust in God to work His will. If a personal wrong has truly been done to us, we seek God in prayer about it, and then leave room for God's judgment and trust Him to do what is best. That is the way to be at peace with God and all men (Romans 12:17-21).

Effective Prayer

The first thing we need to understand about effective prayer is that our Lord and Savior Jesus Christ had to suffer and die on the cross to even make it possible for us to approach the throne of grace to worship and pray (Hebrews 10:19-25). Although the Bible offers a great deal of guidance on how we can deepen our communication with the Creator, effective prayer has more to do with the one doing the praying than it does with "how" we are to pray.

Indeed, Scripture says, "The prayer of a righteous man is powerful and effective" (James 5:16 and that the "eyes of the Lord are on the righteous and his ears are attentive to their prayer" (1 Peter 3:12; Psalm 34:15), and again, "the prayer of the upright pleases Him" (Proverbs 15:8).

Prayer saved the righteous Daniel from the lion's den (Daniel 6:11), and in the wilderness, God's chosen people benefitted from Moses' right standing with God (Exodus 16–17).

The barren Hannah's steadfast and humble prayers resulted in the prophet Samuel (1 Samuel 1:20), and the apostle Paul's prayers even caused the earth to shake (Acts 16:25-26). Clearly, the passionate prayers of God's righteous children can accomplish much (Numbers 11:2).

We need to make sure our prayers are in line with God's will.

"This is the confidence we have in approaching God: that if we ask anything according to His will, he hears us." 1 John 5:14-15.

Praying in accordance with God's will is essentially praying in accord with what He would want, and we can see God's revealed will throughout Scripture. If we do not know what to pray for, Paul reminds us that as God's children, we can rely on the Holy Spirit to intercede for us, as "the Spirit intercedes for the saints in accordance with God's will" (Romans 8:27). And since the Spirit of God knows the mind of God, the Spirit's prayer is always in keeping with the will of the Father.

Additionally, prayer is something believers should do "continually" (1 Thessalonians 5:17). In Luke 18:1, for example, we are told to pray with persistence and "not give up." Also, when we present our requests to God, we are to pray with faith (James 1:5; Mark 11:22-24), with thanksgiving (Philippians 4:6), with a spirit of forgiveness toward others (Mark 11:25), in Christ's name (John 14:13-14), and as stated above, with a heart that is right with God (James 5:16). It is the strength of our faith, not the length of our prayers that pleases Him to whom we pray, so we do not need to impress God with our eloquence or intelligence. After all, God knows what our needs are even before we ask (Matthew 6:8). Effective prayer is a way to strengthen our relationship with our Father in heaven. When we study and obey His Word and seek to please Him, the same God who made the sun stand still upon the prayer of Joshua (Joshua 10:12-13) invites us to come boldly before the throne of grace and pray with confidence that He will extend His mercy and grace to help us in our time of need (Hebrews 4:16).

Obviously, to pray unceasingly cannot mean we are to pray out loud all of the time. Rather, it means we are to be in a constant state of God-consciousness, where we take every thought captive to Him (2 Corinthians 10:5) and bring every situation, plan, fear or concern before His throne. Part of unceasing prayer will be prayers that are spoken, whispered, shouted, sung and silent as we direct our thoughts of praise, petition, supplication and thanksgiving to God.

Pray for our Leaders

> Paul wrote, "I urge, then, first of all, that petitions, prayers, intercession and thanksgiving be made for all people–for kings and all those in authority, that we may live peaceful and quiet lives in all godliness and holiness. This is good, and pleases God our Savior, who wants all people to be saved and to come to a knowledge of the truth." Timothy 2:1–4

God told the Israelites in exile to pray for Babylon:

> "Seek the peace and prosperity of the city to which I have carried you into exile. Pray to the LORD for it, because if it prospers, you too will prosper." Jeremiah 29:7

"Let everyone be subject to the governing authorities, for there is no authority except that which God has established. The authorities that exist have been established by God." Romans 13:1

Paul requested prayer "for all the Lord's people" and for himself that he would speak the gospel boldly (Ephesians 2:18–20).

We do not pray for our leaders simply by command. Praying for them makes practical sense. Our leaders can affect the conditions we live in and have an impact on our families, our churches, our workplaces, our cities and our countries. When those in authority obey the will of God, it is easier to "live peaceful and quiet lives in all godliness and holiness" (1 Timothy 2:2). When evil men are in authority, our prayers for them are just as needed.

Also, we do not pray for our leaders merely for our own benefit. Leadership can be a tiring task.

"Not many of you should become teachers, my fellow believers, because you know that we who teach will be judged more strictly." James 3:1

Leaders carry a degree of responsibility for their followers. They are often the targets of criticism and the go-to people in a crisis. If they lead well, they live their lives in service. We pray for them because we recognize the greatness of their task and because we are grateful for their willingness to lead.

So how should we pray for our leaders? First, if we are uncertain they know Jesus, we should pray for their salvation. But, whether or not our leaders are Christians, we should pray that God will guide them as they guide us. We should pray that they be wise and discerning and surrounded by helpful advisors. We know that God has placed our leaders in authority over us (Romans 13:1), and we can ask Him to use them as He will.

We should also pray for their protection. When praying for pastors or ministry leaders, we can pray for them to have strength in the midst of spiritual warfare and to remain encouraged in the Lord. We can pray for their families, who often feel scrutinized and bear an extra load. Briefly stated, we should mention our leaders before God in prayer and ask Him to have His way in their hearts, to support those around them, and to use their leadership to benefit their followers.

Prayer of Supplication

When we think of supplication, a few things come to mind: entreaty, petition, appeal, request, plea and solicitation. All of these represent prayer. Therefore, all prayers are prayers of supplication. We are to take our requests to God.

> "Do not be anxious about anything, but in everything by prayer and supplication with thanksgiving let your requests be made known to God." Philippians 4:6

Part of winning the spiritual battle is to be "praying at all times in the Spirit, with all prayer and supplication" (Ephesians 6:18).

Prayer of Faith

> *"And the prayer of faith will save the one who is sick, and the Lord will raise him up." James 5:15*

In this context, prayer is offered in faith for someone who is sick, asking God to heal. When we pray, we are to believe in the power and goodness of God (Mark 9:23). Hebrews 11:6 is one of the most compelling reasons why we must have faith when we pray. And without faith, it is impossible to please God, because anyone who comes to him must believe he exists and that he rewards those who earnestly seek him.

Invocation Prayer

An invocation prayer is a request for the spiritual presence and blessing of God in a ceremony or event. To invoke is to call upon earnestly, so an "invocation" in the context of prayer is a serious, intentional calling upon God. It is common for prayers of invocation to be offered publicly at the beginning of a church service or other Christian gathering. Such prayers call upon God to grant His presence in the worship, to bless the service or activity, and to hear the prayers of petition offered to Him.

The Book of Psalms is full of prayers of invocation. Many times, David prayed for God to be present with him and to hear his prayers, particularly in times of trouble and persecution. When David was in danger of being betrayed to King Saul by his enemies, he invoked God's attention to his prayers: "Hear my prayer, O God; listen to the words of my mouth" (Psalm 54:2). Also, in times of deep affliction, David invoked God's presence: "Listen to my prayer, O God, do not ignore my plea" (Psalm 55:1). "Hear my cry, O God; listen to my prayer" (Psalm 61:1).

David's prayers of invocation also begged God to help him in times of trouble. In a prayer that includes elements of imprecation, David invoked God's presence and help against his enemies in Psalm 71:12–13: "Do not be far from me, my God; come quickly, God, to help me. May my accusers perish in shame; may those who want to harm me be covered with scorn and disgrace." Psalm 79:9 invokes God's help for the glory of His name: "Help us, God our Savior, for the glory of your name; deliver us and forgive our sins for your name's sake." David also offered an invocation for God's blessing in a song of praise in Psalm 67:1: "May God be gracious to us and bless us and make his face shine on us."

In what is known as The Lord's Prayer (Matthew 6:9–15), Jesus begins with an invocation that:

1. Identifies God and our relationship to Him: "Our Father in heaven"

2.   Ascribes glory and honor to God: "Hallowed be Your name"

3.   Lines up the petitioner with God's will: "Your kingdom come. Your will be done on earth as it is in heaven."

As Christians, we have access to the throne of God through faith in Christ (Ephesians 3:12). All our prayers of invocation should contain the elements of humility, praise and reverence as we approach, in Jesus' name, the One whose blessing we seek.

Prayer of Thanksgiving

We see another type of prayer in Philippians 4:5: thanksgiving or thanks to God. "With thanksgiving let your requests be made known to God." Many examples of thanksgiving prayers can be found in the Psalms. We should include thanks in all of our prayers. Thanks for everything God has done, is doing and will do.

Prayer of Worship

The prayer of worship is similar to the prayer of thanksgiving. The difference is that worship focuses on who God is; thanksgiving focuses on what God has done. Church leaders in Antioch prayed in this manner with fasting:

"While they were worshiping the Lord and fasting, the Holy Spirit said, 'Set apart for me Barnabas and Saul for the work to which I have called them.' Then after fasting and praying they laid their hands on them and sent them off." Acts 13:2-3

Prayer of Consecration

Sometimes, prayer is a time of setting ourselves apart to follow God's will. Jesus made such a prayer the night before His crucifixion:

"And going a little farther He fell on his face and prayed, saying, 'My Father, if it be possible, let this cup pass from me; nevertheless, not as I will, but as you will.'" Matthew 26:39

The Bible reveals many types of prayers and employs a variety of words to describe the practice. For example:

"First of all, then, I urge that supplications, prayers, intercessions, and thanksgivings be made for all people." 1 Timothy 2:1

Here, all four of the main Greek words used for prayer are mentioned in one verse.

DISCUSSION QUESTIONS

1. Why do you think there are different types of prayers?
2. Why is the imprecatory prayer one that should be done with the most care, understanding and wisdom from God?
3. What is your understanding of the sinners prayer?
4. When you pray the prayer of worship, should you be in corporate prayer or alone, or both? Why?
5. Think about the type of praying that you do. Which of the descriptions listed fit most of your prayers? How can you incorporate other types of prayers in your prayer life?

CHAPTER 7: PUSH–PRAY UNTIL SOMETHING HAPPENS

"I cried to him with my mouth, and high praise was on my tongue." Psalm 66:17

"Let us come into his presence with thanksgiving; let us make a joyful noise to him with songs of praise!" Psalm 95:2

"After this manner therefore pray ye: Our Father which art in heaven, Hallowed be thy name. Thy kingdom come, Thy will be done in earth, as it is in heaven. Give us this day our daily bread. And forgive us our debts, as we forgive our debtors. And lead us not into temptation, but deliver us from evil: For thine is the kingdom, and the power, and the glory, forever. Amen." (KJV) Matthew 6:9-13

"What am I to do? I will pray with my spirit, but I will pray with my mind also; I will sing praise with my spirit, but I will sing with my mind also." 1 Corinthians 14:15

"But let him ask in faith, with no doubting, for the one who doubts is like a wave of the sea that is driven and tossed by the wind." James 1:6

Prayer is one of the greatest powers available in the entire universe. Prayer goes into the spiritual realm, bringing things out of that unseen realm and into the world around us, right where we live. It ushers spiritual blessings into our natural, everyday lives and brings spiritual power to bear on our earthly circumstances. We as human beings are the only creatures in our known universe who can stand in the natural realm and touch the spiritual realm. When we pray, we connect with God, and He affects our daily lives beyond comprehension. Prayer opens the door for God to work. It is the activity you and I can engage in on Earth when we need the power of heaven to come into our lives to bring wisdom, direction, encouragement or a miraculous breakthrough. Prayer connects us to the power of God–and that is why it is a greater force than anything else we can ever imagine.

Only the power of prayer can move the hand of God. And only the power of God can change an individual heart, free a person from bondage and torment, overturn disappointments and devastations, break an addiction, or heal a person's emotions. Only God's power can bring peace, instill joy, grant wisdom, impart a sense of value and purpose to a person who does not know what to do in life, and work every kind of miracle.

Insincere prayer cannot be a substitute for justice and responsible action. Ultimately, the believer is impelled to pray by the indwelling God at work in the deepest places of his or her soul.

You see, the real Christian experience is not a feeling but a relationship based on trust–or faith. The Bible records many experiences that followers of Jesus encountered, but the fundamental experience of a relationship with God is trust–or faith–in Jesus. Faith is always "in" something, you just do not "have faith," you have faith in something. Faith is always "for" something, it looks forward to an outcome. Faith does not always have the same feeling associated with it, and may sometimes not feel like anything at all. The evidence that you are a Christian is that you trust Jesus, not that you have any particular feeling.

Now, praying to Jesus is an exercise of faith in Jesus. Do you trust that Jesus hears your prayers? Do you trust that Jesus answers your prayers? And do you trust that Jesus loves you? God hears our prayers and answers them (though not always in the way, or with the timing, we might expect). I know this, not because of how I feel after I have prayed, but because I trust in the promises that God makes to us in the Bible.

http://christianity.net.au/questions/how_do_i_know_if_my_prayers_really_work

One of the most wonderful mysteries in the universe is that prayer changes things. God has arranged his world for us to have the ability to make significant choices some good, some bad–which affect the course of history. God has given us the act of prayer–asking him to act–to accomplish this. Because He is all-wise and all-powerful, knowing "the end from the beginning" (Isa. 46:10), He is able to weave our requests into His eternally good purposes. It is always foolish and dangerous to play up one aspect of what the Bible teaches at the expense of something else it equally affirms. The God of the Bible is presented as the one who rules over all; he is all-knowing, all-wise and all-powerful. He is not surprised by anything we may think or do.

On the other hand, Scripture presents human beings as responsible moral agents who make significant choices, doing what we desire to do–freedom of inclination. God has chosen to relate to us personally without compromising the fact that he is God.

Scripture describes the sovereign God as "repenting" or "relenting" in response to human prayer. In Exodus 32, Moses appeals to God as the sovereign king to show mercy (vv. 11-13). And that is exactly what happens:

> *"Then the LORD relented and did not bring on his people the disaster he had threatened." (v. 14).*

Our problem in trying to see how prayer works is that we often have a wrong view of God in relation to His world. God has the power and wisdom to use our prayers as He sees best and to do what we could never imagine. If He were not all-powerful, there would be little point in praying. If He were not all-wise, it would be dangerous to pray; after all, who would want to ask an all-powerful but foolish person to do anything? God is perfectly wise and infinitely powerful, which is why you and I can pray with confidence.

https://www.thegospelcoalition.org/article/why-prayer-changes-things

Both the prayer and the answer to the prayer were ordained by God. This explains how prayer can have real results and how God can be sovereign at the same time. God ordains the end result and God ordains your prayer as the means of getting to that end result. Why does God choose to work this way? Why not just do everything Himself? Why include us? I believe the answer is so that His people can be involved in His work and thus be drawn closer to Him.

Next time you pray, think to yourself, "This prayer really matters. God has ordained that I pray. He intends to change me through my prayer, and He has ordained that my prayer be put to some good purpose in the world–to bring about a good result."

If God has already ordained that something will happen, does it really matter whether or not I pray for it to happen? The answer is emphatically, "Yes, it does matter!" And here is why.

God ordains ends and God ordains means. For example, when God ordains that a Tabernacle be built, He calls and gifts two men named Bezalel and Oholiab to build it (Exodus 35:30-35). When God ordains that Cornelius, the Gentile hear the gospel for the first time, He sends the Apostle Peter to tell him the gospel (Acts 10; cf. Romans 10:13-15).

To use the example of Elijah from James 5, above: God ordains the ends (that the rain will stop) and He ordains the means (Elijah's fervent prayer for the rain to stop). Elijah's prayer was indeed effective to stop the rain. God really did answer his prayer.

http://www.christiananswers.net/q-aiia/aiia-whypray.html

Therefore, praying until something happens is imperative. This means you keep praying until you see the results of your prayer. God will reveal His answer if your heart and mind are open to Him. Keep your eyes, mind, and heart focused on God and your faith unwavering and you will know that your prayer is answered. This answer will lead you to more prayer and a better prayer life.

DISCUSSION QUESTIONS

1. Explain how prayer can have real results.
2. What does repenting and relenting mean in reference to prayer?
3. What are some attributes of God that help us know that He will change things that we pray for?
4. Why do you think the power of prayer can move the hand of God?
5. What do you think the words "Pray until something happens" mean?

CHAPTER 8: CONCLUSION

Now that you've come this far, has your view of prayer changed? What will be your takeaway? First and foremost, your understanding of what prayer is, why you should pray, and what hinders your prayer life should be top of recall. And next, you should know that you should always pray. When you pray until something happens, you are praying with faith and knowing that God not only hears your prayers but He also answers them. You will continue to pray and be careful to make your request known to God and believe that He will do what is right and it will be done at the right time.

Powerful Points of Prayer

Prayer is a communication with God.

Communication is a conversation that involves both talking and listening. Some people have problems in knowing if God is answering their prayer or if it is just the way life is. The best way to know God's answers is to study His Word. All of the answers you need can be found there.

Prayer is a dialogue not a monologue.

God answers us in many ways and if we know Him and His Word then we are sure to see the answers. Every one of us can pray. We don't have to be fine orators or have all the right words and intonations. God only requires a willing and believing heart. Prayer is important in the lives of everyone, but especially to Christians who know, trust and believe in the true and living God.

Prayer is a perpetual exercise of faith.

Each time you pray, you exercise your faith that God will answer you.

Prayer is a commandment of God.

We should pray to Him because he is willing and able to supply our every need. We also should pray to thank Him for what He has done, what He is doing now and what He will do in the future. Why we pray:

> "Watch and pray so that you will not fall into temptation. The spirit is willing, but the flesh is weak." Matt 26: 41.

According to this scripture, you are not only commanded to pray, but to watch. To watch is to ensure two things, first that you know God's will and second that you are not praying outside of God's will. Remain in the spirit of God and you will pray as you should.

> "Only ask, and I will give you the nations as your inheritance, the ends of the earth as your possession." Psalms 2:8, NLT

You know what the Great Commission is.

As a true believer in Jesus, you are mandated to carry it out. When you do this, you see change over the circumstances you are praying for. We discover our mandate from Christ in such a command:

> "Therefore go and make disciples of all nations...teaching them to obey everything I have commanded you." Mathew. 28:19-20, NIV

Luke provides a description of the biblical pattern for fulfilling this mandate when he tells in his gospel how the early church responded to Christ's command:

> "Day after day, in the temple courts and from house to house, they never stopped teaching and proclaiming the good news that Jesus is the Christ." Acts 5:42

God is in charge of this world. So, for us to have answers to prayer, we must pray His will.

> "Verily I say unto you, Whatsoever ye shall bind on earth shall be bound in heaven: and whatsoever ye shall loose on earth shall be loosed in heaven." Mathew 18:18.

> 23God never does anything against His will. The Holy Spirit works within us to help us what we can and should bind and what we can and should loose. 24Whoever does not love Me does not keep My words. The word that you hear is not My own, but it is from the Father who sent Me. 25All this I have spoken to you while I am still with you. 26But the Advocate, the Holy Spirit, whom the Father will send in My name, will teach you all things and will remind you of everything I have told you. Peace I leave with you; my peace I give you. I do not give to you as the world gives. Do not let your hearts be troubled and do not be afraid… John 14:24-27

When we walk in the Spirit, the Lord waits for us to decree and then He establishes. The most important thing to note is that God is all-powerful, all-knowing and the only wise God.

Prayer is not just to ask for the needs we have.

God already knows what we need and He tells us clearly in Isaiah 65:24, "I will answer them before they even call to me.

While they are still talking about their needs, I will go ahead and answer their prayers!"

Prayer is designed to help us become into fellowship with God. Jesus died and opened the door to communion with God. As we pray with the leading of the Holy Spirit, we are in that fellowship. Prayer is fellowship with God.

"Men ought always to pray," can then be seen as "Men ought always to fellowship with God."

Prayer without faith is in vain.

When you pray, you must pray with the expectation that God will answer your prayer according to His will and timing. You must have faith in God and that your prayer will be heard and answered. God delights in our prayer, even though He knows what you need before you ask. He delights in knowing that you love, respect and have enough faith in Him to come to His throne of grace and make a petition to Him. Jesus did not ask us to pray for the sake of praying as a Christian routine, but He asks us to pray so that we can receive. You will not pray vain repetition even when you repeat yourself. Your prayer will be embedded with faith in Jesus that He hears and answers prayer. As we spend time in fellowship with the Lord, all the works of the evil one are exposed and we can walk in the Light of God. For he that walks in the light shall fear no evil. For the Light of the Lord shines in darkness, and the darkness cannot comprehend it (John 1:5). If we walk in the light, then there is no darkness in us (I John 1:5-7). The Bible says we should be sober; we should watch and pray, for the enemy goes about like a roaring lion. If we are in the fellowship of our Lord we can anticipate the devil's act and defeat it.

The Lord is our shield and defense. He knows all about the works of the evil one and will expose them to us if we are in fellowship with Him. If we walk with Him, we walk in the newness of life. Prayer should be offensive and not just defensive; let us destroy the works of the enemy in prayer. The devil fears a God-fearing Christian that is in constant fellowship with the Lord. If we keep an attitude of prayer and walk in the Spirit, we destroy the plans of the evil one. God wants you to learn to pray more effectively, and He wants your prayer life to become more fulfilling. People of prayer, in your faithfulness to voluntarily spend time in prayer on behalf of others, we can experience transformation of our families, cities and nations if we are will be willing to labor together. When you send a bold, humble prayer in faith heavenward. You can repeat it as often as you must until you get the answer. It does not mean you can't pray more than once for the same thing. Jesus says "knock"– and keep knocking. Prayer should be made continuously without ceasing. In any particular request, we should keep asking, reminding God until our joy is full. That is faith repetition–not vain repetition. Keep the Word of God in total obedience, keep the faith and keep praying until your joy is full.

There are many types of prayers, but they all begin and end with faith in God and His ability to hear and answer each one. The Bible reveals various forms of prayers and employs an abundance of words to describe the practice.

"First of all, then, I urge that supplications, prayers, intercessions, and thanksgivings be made for all people." 1 Timothy 2:1

Here, all four of the main Greek words used for prayer are mentioned in one verse.

We are the only creatures in our known universe who can stand in the natural realm and touch the spiritual realm. When we pray, we connect with God, and He affects our daily lives beyond comprehension. The Holy Spirit leads us, teaches us and guides us to overcome these hindrances, if we ask Him to help us in our daily Christian walk with Jesus Christ.

As you will recall, hinder means to delay, deter, hamper, encumber, obstruct, thwart, impede, hold back or get in the way. All of these synonyms are negative, and when we allow something to hinder our prayer life, we allow the enemy to steal our joy. Our prayers are often hindered. While we can be sure that God hears our prayers, there are times when He chooses not to heed or answer them. You are the only one who can hinder your prayers. God delays His answers, so that we can seek Him, and also learn how to be patient.

Both the prayer and the answer to the prayer were ordained by God. This explains how prayer can have real results and God can be sovereign at the same time. God ordains the end result and God ordains your prayer as the means of getting to that end result.

Scripture to Remember

1 I urge, then, first of all, that petitions, prayers, intercession and thanksgiving be made for all people— 2 for kings and all those in authority, that we may live peaceful and quiet lives in all godliness and holiness. 3 This is good, and pleases God our Savior, 4 who wants all people to be saved and to come to a knowledge of the truth. 1 Timothy 2:1-4 (NIV)

DISCUSSION QUESTIONS

Chapter 1

1. What is your definition of prayer?
2. Why do you need to search the scriptures to discover effective praying?
3. Is a simple prayer just as effective as a long prayer? Why or Why Not?
4. Why is prayer a dialogue and not a monologue?
5. Should all prayers follow the model of The Lord's Prayer? Why or Why Not?
6. Why is daily prayer a must to have a complete prayer life?

Chapter 2

1. Why pray?
2. What are three reasons why you should pray?
3. What does it mean to have your spirit aligned with God's spirit?
4. What is genuine preparation?
5. What does prayer ministry mean to you?

Chapter 3

1. Does praying take anything away from God and who and what He is?
2. Name three ways you can know that your prayers are answered.
3. What does repenting and relenting mean in relation to how God answers prayers?
4. Why do feelings have nothing to do with how God answers our prayers?

5. Why does fulfilling the mandate of the Great Commission always involve a prayer life?

Chapter 4

1. What does vain repetition mean to you? Give an example.
2. Why did Jesus warn against vain repetition?
3. Do you think asking God over and over for the same thing is vain repetition? Why or why not?
4. What does John 14:13-16 mean to you?
5. Why is it important to have faith when praying?

Chapter 5

1. What are three things that hinder prayer? Explain how they hinder prayer.
2. Why does an unforgiving heart hinder prayer?
3. What can you do to ensure that you are not praying alone?
4. How does forgetting the poor create a disconnect between you and God?
5. Why should you wait on the answers from God?
6. Can you think of other ways that prayers can be hindered? If so, what are they?
7. How does an unthankful heart hinder prayer? Explain your answer thoroughly.

Chapter 6

1. Why do you think there are different types of prayers?
2. Why is the imprecatory prayer one that should be done with the most care, understanding, and wisdom from god?
3. What is your understanding of the sinners prayer?
4. When you pray the prayer of worship, should you be in corporate prayer, alone, or both? Why?

5. Think about the type of praying you do. Which of the descriptions listed describe most of your prayers? How can you incorporate other types of prayers in your prayer life?

Chapter 7

1. Explain how prayer can have real results.
2. What does repenting and relenting mean in reference to prayer?
3. What are some attributes of God that help us to know He will change things that we pray for?
4. Why do you think the power of prayer can move the hand of God?
5. What do you think the words "pray until something happens" mean?

OVERALL GENERAL QUESTIONS

1. What is the difference between persistence in prayer and pestering God, because you are not sure He will answer?
2. When does the positive persistence turn into pestering petitions?
3. Does Satan hear our prayers when we pray aloud and try to find ways, other than making me sleepy when praying–to thwart my answers?
4. When we pray for others, are they also required to pray if the prayer is only for them?
5. Should you expect others to pray for you when they ask you to pray for them? Why or why not?

REFERENCES

biblestudytools.com/encyclopedias/isbe/prayer.html

http://christianity.net.au/questions/how_do_i_know_if_my_prayers_really_work http://www.christiananswers.net/q-aiia/aiia-whypray.html http://www.dictionary.com/browse/prayer

Norman Geisler, *Systematic Theology: Volume 2: God, Creation* (Bethany House, 2003)

http://www.gospelchapel.com/Devotions/11_98/devotion_11-04-98.html

https://www.thegospelcoalition.org/article/why-prayerchanges-things merriam-webster.com/dictionary/prayer

http://www.theopedia.com/transcendence-of-god

http://thinkexist.com/quotation/pray_oftenfor_prayer_is_a_shield_to_the_soul-a/197223.html

About The Author

Ms. Farley is a retired teacher and lives by the motto "Jesus Christ is the head of my life". She began writing stories in the first grade and has not stopped writing since.

Having retired from 37 years of teaching in the publicschool systems of the South, Ms. Farley has learned the power of prayer by experience.

She has discovered after traveling extensively on the North American continent that time spent with the giver outweighs even the gift.

The author has gone down the road of accumulating wealth. She watches TV, works on her computer, and enjoys popular music, in other words she is a real person.
Prayer is for real people like her and you.

OTHER BOOKS BY MARIER FARLEY

Stranger In Town

To Love Wisely

Twice Shy

A Father For Me, Meghan

They Knew How To Cook

It's Time to Move

One Last Thing...

If you enjoyed this book or found it useful I'd be very grateful if you'd post a short review on Amazon. Your support really does make a difference and I read all the reviews personally so I can get your feedback and make this book even better.

If you'd like to leave a review then all you need to do is click the review link on this book's page on Amazon.

Thanks again for your support!

Thanks to all of my beta readers for help making these stories possible. Without you they would only be out of my head. Now your heads are involved as well. Once the book goes live please take a minute to leave a review on amazon.com and my website www.marierfarley.com

12981094R00049

Made in the USA
Middletown, DE
24 November 2018